PIMPS, PLAYAS, & VIRTUE SLAYERS

by Susan Horton

authorHOUSE®

AuthorHouse™
1663 Liberty Drive
Bloomington, IN 47403
www.authorhouse.com
Phone: 1-800-839-8640

Published by AuthorHouse 12/19/2012

ISBN: 978-1-4817-0083-2 (sc)
ISBN: 978-1-4817-0082-5 (e)

Library of Congress Control Number: 2012923816

The Pimps...

A pimp by definition is one who sells the company of women for a price, but in all actuality, a pimp is someone who will do anything...I do mean A-NEE-THING to get some money. He will perform the tricks himself in order to get what really drives him. He is a weak individual who brags about how much he loves his mother, but treats other women with total disdain. This type of man also leases his services of protection and guidance to this same woman who is indebted to him and fulfills her obligation by sleeping with other men to repay it.

A pimp has one true love and that is money. The clothes, the cars, and the fancy colognes are tools of the trade. It is merely flash and an illusion of security. Truth be told, this man is mentally, socially, emotionally and spiritually drained. He is a shell of a man who is trying to fulfill an empty existence with things and a faux financial status. He herds empty women into stables of carnal pleasure, and even though he will persuade this woman to work for him and convince her that they are a team, he is only interested in the dough.

This definition is a common understanding and has been the norm for centuries. This story however will take a look at pimping from another angle. For so long women have been taken advantage of by some man who is in it for all he can get out of her. He will pretend to love her and pretend that he has her back all in the hopes that she will take care of him financially.

There are countless women who will settle for this treatment because they feel they have nothing else and will not get anyone else if they let this loser go. This is how the pimp is able to keep her in check. The old fashion pimp uses brute force, mind games, or drugs to keep his ladies in check, but an emotional pimp uses loneliness and low self esteem to corral his lover and keep her in his debt. She will do anything to keep him and he knows it.

PIMPS

HI MY NAME IS WANDA and I want to share my story. I had had it with the brothahs…not your mother's son, but men of color, so I decided to explore the rainbow and see what else was out there. I hadn't had any better luck with other races until one day I was walking along eating my favorite hot wings and chucking the bones out as I strolled thru Allie's Park. When I heard the most peculiar voice say:

"Hey beautiful lady! Hey you! You might want to stop doing that." I turned with the entire sistah girl within me; prepared to read him up one side and down the other and looked into the brightest smile I had ever seen in my life. I mean this guys teeth would have made those Colgate teeth go somewhere and sit down. He was cute in an intellectual sort of way. He kind of reminded me of a cross between The Rock and Mr. Rogers. Nonetheless, those teeth softened my heart and I offered him a sweet hello.

"You're too pretty to be a litter bug, so let me get those for you." He adjusted his pace to match mine and then proceeded to catch every bone as I finished gobbling it up. Another woman might have just sat down and eaten her lunch, but this was my time and he was intruding. I didn't feel the need to change my plans because he wanted some company.

"My name is Stanford." I looked at him like he was literally from Mars. I didn't want to know his name nor was I interested in where this was going. I had been down this road too many times with brothahs and I don't want to make the journey back from where it leads. They waltz into your life unexpectedly, and flash those vampire like smiles and then drain every bit of love from your life before moving on to the next victim.

"Stanford thanks for giving a hoot whether or not I pollute. I have to get back to work now. I will be seeing you around." I turned and began walking away without so much as a wave goodbye. He didn't get the memo on that, because he then proceeded to follow me.

"Look man; are you some kind of stalker or something?" I was totally perturbed. I wanted this jerk to disappear and do it quickly.

"Wow! Somebody did a number on you." I turned around and looked at this PBS reject with smoke coming out of my ears. How dare he? Who the hell did he think he was talking to like that?

"Look honey, I don't have any spare change nor am I interested in what you are selling." Again I started walking away. I couldn't believe the nerve of this fool. He is going to make me call Tyrone and 'nem. That's the problem with men. They think they know everything.

"You are too beautiful to be so bitter. I just thought I would make your day, that's all. Go on and get a ticket for littering. Those fines are a killer." He still stood there with this goofy grin on his face. I was somewhat attracted to his smile.

"Wanda." I gave him a half smile as a peace offering. I then extended my hand to let him know I was sorry for being so difficult at our meeting.

"Excuse me?" He looked completely confused.

"Wanda. My name is Wanda Tyler." He then returned the half smile and met my hand with a kiss. This gave him a few more points. He took a handkerchief out of his pocket and dusted off a bench and invited me to sit and talk with him.

"So Mrs. Tyler what do you do besides spread litter?"

I met his corny comment by smiling and correcting his obvious attempt at fishing for information. "It's Miss Tyler."

"A charming woman like you is still lingering on the vine? Impossible!" He was still obvious, but I must admit it was working.

"I wouldn't say lingering…just getting sweeter by the day. When I get nice and ripe the right man will come along and pluck this berry." I threw my head back with pride. I was only 32, but I looked damn good for my age. I worked out 5 times a week, I had flawless skin and I had the legs of a super model. Any man would be grateful to get me in his basket.

"I must admit I have this thing for black berries." He looked at me and licked his lips. He looked mighty thirsty and I was the cool dip he needed to quench it. I made the decision months ago to start dating other races of people, and this would be the first time that I acted on it. I went out with a Latino, but he was looking for a quick fix and that is never on my agenda. I hadn't had the privilege of dating an Asian or a Native American, but I figured that I needed to start somewhere.

He then did the most disrespectful thing that he could have done. He hugged himself in one of those rapper-like poses and then said;"Won't you be my smoofie girl!!"

I got up and stormed away. If I was interested in being entertained by a clown, I would have stayed with that last joker I was with. He started to run behind me, but I was determined to get away from him. I ducked into the nearest Starbucks.

"Hey wait a minute! Did I do something wrong?" I looked at this goofball and decided that he couldn't be that clueless. How dare you put on an inside out minstrel show and think that you did nothing wrong. I just shook my head and stood in line like I didn't know him.

"I'll have a green tea latte…uh grande please." I sat my purse on the counter and proceeded to search for my wallet. He jumps in front of me and hands the clerk a twenty dollar bill.

"It's okay. I got this." I looked at this lunatic and continued to search for my billfold.

"I'm fine." I found it, but he blocked me when I pulled out my debit card.

"It's okay…let me pay. It will be my way of apologizing." He then flashed those choppers. I nodded and added a slice of vanilla bean cheesecake. Not that I ate that kind of junk, I just wanted to make him pay a little more for that slip up. The clerk handed me the tea and he took the tray with the cheesecake on it and then found us a table.

"I guess you don't like smoothies. My bad." I just looked at his attempt at some swagger. It was kind of charming. I must admit he had warmed my heart. So I obliged his corny chatter.

"No, they have too many calories and too many different ingredients. I like it plain and simple…no chaser." I said with a matter of fact tone in my voice. We sat there for the rest of my lunch hour exchanging first date banter and then he did the most peculiar thing.

"I have to go." He then got up and began to walk away without saying goodbye.

"Wait!" I jumped up and ran after him. "Wait a minute!"

He continued to walk as quickly as he could and then he turned the corner and disappeared. I stopped dead in my tracks and started to turn the other way. I was so confused.

Weren't we having a good time? Maybe I was just so happy to have a decent conversation where I didn't have to dumb myself down until I made it out to be more than it was. I started back towards my building just as confused as ever. What was really going on? Oh well. I can't believe I spent my lunch hour engaging this stranger, and what had I said or done to drive him away? I thought I had met someone I could be with for a while. This serves me right for having any expectations of love.

The next two days passed and I heard nothing from this mysterious stranger. I thought about him a lot and wondered what could have been said or done to cause him to respond to me that way. What if I offended him with my attitude? I have a tendency to do that. In the past, I have isolated my share of men with my sho'nuff mentality. Men don't want to date an attitude; they want you to be soft and caring.

Well a week had passed since I met this perfect stranger. I had begun to put him out of my mind when all of a sudden he reappears out of nowhere. I am at the Starbucks ordering my favorite latte and guess who saunters up next to me?

"Add a vanilla bean cheesecake to that please." He grinned as he plopped down a twenty dollar bill. I was excited and relieved at the same time to see him. I didn't even acknowledge his presence. I picked up my latte and walked right out the door. I felt vindicated. I strolled to nearest park bench and slurped with pride. I saw this joker walking towards me with that dreadful cheesecake in his hand.

"I guess you wanted that to go." He chimed in his own little corny way.

I rolled my eyes and continued to sip my drink. In between gulps I managed a simple, "Get lost."

"Listen, listen, I'm sorry…it's just that…" He stops in mid sentence. He clears his throat and continues. "It's just that I was reminded of how much I have been missing since I lost my wife a year ago. She was all I had and now that she's gone I never thought I could ever meet someone who could make me forget the pain and it scared me." I looked into his eyes for a shred of sincerity and I found that and more. He was tearing up and that pricked my heart. I instinctively began to comfort him, so much so that we spent the next couple of hours at the nearest motel. I knew I was a fool for giving it up so easy but I felt like this somehow was going to be different.

"So tell me what happened?" I asked as I was putting my clothes back on.

He looked me square in the eye with the most peculiar glare. If I didn't know better, I would think he was telling me to mind my own business with his eyes. Instead he sat up on the side of the bed and looked at a corner of the room where the window was.

"My wife and I got married too soon. We were both too young to get married, but she was so beautiful until I couldn't leave that bar without her. She had the body of a goddess and danced like an angel." He stood up and walked to the sink. He began to wash his face and dry it with the towel hanging on the side of the wall.

"What happened? Did she…" before I could finish my statement. He interrupted me.

"When she divorced me, I was devastated. I didn't expect that would ever happen. We were so happy, or at least I thought we were. Then out of the blue she just up and leaves me for someone else." He continued to talk as if I were no longer in the room. "That was the worst day in my life. I have never gotten over her…I mean that." He looked at me to gauge my reaction. I didn't trip because I know a few rules of thumb. Never be jealous of the memory. It was what it was. Let him have that besides you are there now.

"I can imagine. We never forget old loves, but the best

way to forget an old one is to get yourself a new one." I walk up to him and grab his chest from behind. He places his hands over mine and turns himself around to look me in the face. He cups my cheeks with his strong hands and then smiles. He placed his mouth over mine and gently kissed as if he was a wound vampire and he was sucking the life out of all my past hurts. His kiss removed memories from loves lost and unsuccessful relationships. I surrendered my heart to him at that moment and vowed to be there for him.

We became inseparable after that day...well we saw as much of each other as our respective jobs allowed. He would disappear for a few days and then show up ravenous for my love. He said that he had to travel out of town and that it took him to some pretty lame places. This was the excuse he gave me when I asked if I could travel with him some times.

MOVING DAY...

Hon, where should we put this statue?" I was trying unsuccessfully to mix our eclectic lives together in our new condo. It was beautiful! A little expensive, but we deserved a new start together. He said we should keep everything in my name since he still had credit issues from his past relationship. She took it all. The money, the house, the car and their time share. He wasn't in a position to get a loan to buy her out so she sold their entire life out from under him. Well there was not going to be a replay with me. I am down for my man and would do anything to make him happy.

"Sweetie where is that box with all the towels in it. I'm feeling really gritty and need a shower." I was tired of trying to decorate. I might have to call in a professional, because this is way out of my league.

"Look in the bedroom." He answered dryly. He was arguing with someone on his cell phone. It looked like he was whispering so I just grabbed the shower gel and my towels and headed for that beautiful bathroom. It was what I have always wanted. There were double sinks with plenty of counter space, a shower stall with all of those water spouts and my pride and joy, a sunken tub. The skyline was just the icing on the cake. I decided to forego the shower and sink into that sunken tub. I light some scented candles and pour in some bath milk. As I watch that tub fill up, I hear a low and inviting voice say, "Want some company?" It was the love of my life.

"You know the answer to that question." I began to slip out of my clothes.

He walked up behind me and began to massage my body with his strong hands. He knew how to touch me and make me melt like butter.

As I melted in his arms, his phone begins to vibrate. He quickly turned his attention from me to it and ran to the floor where his pants were laying and turned it off.

"Now where were we sweetie?" I was so looking forward to what was about to happen next I totally forgot all about the interruption. He returned to the spot he left on my body and continued to massage away the day. As we climbed into that sunken tub, he began to wash my body. He was careful to pay special attention to his favorite areas. He scrubbed and massaged for what seemed like forever. I then returned the favor; stroking and kissing as I went along. We climbed that stair way to heaven until the water turned cold and our skin began to wrinkle. Needless to say, he wasn't finished with me yet. We strolled over to the shower, where he rinsed me off with kisses. First, he took my breasts in his hands and nibbled like I was a source of life for him. Then he journeyed down to my womanhood and found his purpose in me. He kissed in all the right places; his tongue plunging in and out of my love.

I too had a point to prove. I fell to my knees and showed him that he was my king and that I was a willing subject. With every pull, I wanted him to know I would do any and every little thing he asked me too. Just before he spilled that honey, I let go, and gave him a wicked look. Even though we both had clearly established our role in each other's will, this was not over by a long shot. I took a towel from the rack and began to dry him off. Then it appeared that he wasn't quite thru with me yet, because he then threw me on the bed and dove inside my body as if I were the Atlantic. He ferociously stroked as if I were a race he wanted desperately to win. He flipped me in every position we could achieve. Then just before I reached glory, he took out his magic wand and prepared to take me to another level.

He went into our little treasure box and pulled out some Wet and gave me an evil stare. I guess he still had a lesson to teach me. He applied the gel to my rear and as it was preparing me for the inevitable, he put his mouth on my love and began to tickle and tease me. It was more like torture. I grabbed his ears and pulled his head into me as he licked me like an ice cream cone. Then he flipped me over and began to gently ease his manhood into my backdoor. We slid rhythmically together. My arches were reaching up to meet his thrusts until he or I couldn't take any more.

As we spooned, consoling each other from the love fest, I thought about the phone call he received before we began. There had been times when other women had called and he answered right in front of me to keep me from being suspicious. I mean, why even bother? I was the one in his bed every night. I was the one who he leans on when times are rough. It's my arms that comfort him, so what can some other woman give him that I am not already supplying?

While I am going over all of this in my head, he picks up his cell phone and then takes it in the bathroom. I had half a mind to follow him and get a replay, but just before I could get off the bed he closed and locked the door.

"Well go ahead and keep your secrets then." I settled back into our bed and pulled out my calendar for the next day. I had two meetings and a hair appointment scheduled. I would probably be out of the office all day so that will call for a pantsuit. I walked into our closet and perused my wardrobe for just the right attire when I thought I heard a knock at the door. I quickly grabbed my robe and headed for the foyer when he burst out of the bathroom and ran past me.

"Baby, what is going on?" He had been acting strangely for the past two weeks and I was going to get to the bottom of whatever it was.

He opened the door just barely enough to step out of it and then someone on the other side grabbed him and started stomping him.

"Stop it! Stop it! Please don't hurt him!" They were beating him as if it was their mission to kill him.

"Lady back up or we'll give you some too!" I was so frightened. I ran back into the condo to call the police, one of the terrorist followed me and grabbed me from behind. He threw me onto the sofa and pinned my hands to the cushions

"I hate to tell you this baby, but your old man is into us for 20,000 and unless he pays in a week, he is a dead man!" He surveyed my bare breasts and then set me free. I quickly covered myself and sat helplessly on the sofa wept. As the assailants walked out of our life just as boldly as they came, Stanford wandered back into the house and sat next to me.

"All that stuff you claim that your ex took from you...." I didn't even get the chance to finish my statement. He dropped his head and turned away. I shook mine in angst. I knew the other shoe would drop sooner or later.

I jumped up off the sofa and stormed down the hallway.

He tried to come after me, but the beating was too fresh and he was really hurt.

"Good". I thought to myself. This serves him right for bringing all of this drama into my life. I almost wished it were another woman. I was tempted to believe that I had the last good man out there. There is no such a thing as a righteous man. They are all hiding something, whether it is another woman, bad credit, a down-low lifestyle or they are just plain old abusive. Perhaps it's me that is the problem. I just can't seem to find that happily ever after.

Stan eases the door open and lay beside me. I think of the past two months and recognize a pattern in the last 10 years. When the chips are down; I bounce. I don't stick around to let the banner fall. Truth be told, I was already plotting to put this condo on the market in between my last meeting and my hair appointment. As he lay there helpless and weak, I think back to promises we just made to each other in that bathroom. I embrace him and snuggle his neck and wait until morning to make my final decision.

I awake to the smell of eggs, bacon and coffee. I grab a shower, pull my hair back in a bun and dress quickly. Stan meets me at the bottom of the stairs with my favorite cup.

"Come on sweetheart, sit down and have breakfast with me." I take the cup and dump it in my travel mug and mumble a curt goodbye.

"I can't. I have some meetings that may run long, so I will be late." I pick up my briefcase and scurry out the door without so much as kiss. I can't even look his way. I am so damned disappointed in him. I walk out the door and get into my car and pull off so fast that my tires made a screeching sound.

"Damn...guess I am pretty mad. I better slow my behind down before I get a ticket." I was so pre-occupied that I didn't see the car following me until I turned into the garage. An

Audi pulled up next to me as I parked. I busied myself with my briefcase and some papers I had on the seat. I waited until whoever was in the car made their move. Minutes passed and not so much as a door opened on the car next to me. I had to get out eventually so I made my move. I opened my door and leaned back over to get my coffee and briefcase when all of a sudden the driver's side door opened and a female got out. She was tall and blonde and very thin. She could have been a model. I breathed a sigh of relief. I have become totally paranoid. My mind wonders back to Stanford and all that drama he has brought to my life and I get mad all over again.

I get on the elevator of the parking garage and decide that I can't face today in that office. I quickly push the button to open the door and call Monty, my supervisor. I explain to him that I am having some family problems and needed to take a couple of days off. He claims he understands and would see me in two days. He took care to emphasize the word "two". I could always count on Monty to be a dick.

I rush back to my car and make a bee-line for my house. I feel this urgency and I can't describe why. I can't wait to get back there and give Stan a piece of my mind. What I found when I got there words couldn't describe. One of those men who came last night was at my door and as soon as he recognized my car he went into my house.

"What in hell is going on?" I was determined to put an end this mess right now. I storm up the driveway and you would never believe in a million years what I saw. The man I loved, supported, planned to marry was on his knees begging for his life. That was it, I couldn't take this anymore. I would help him get out of this mess, but after that he would have to leave my life. I didn't sign up for this madness.

"What does he owe you?" I reached for my checkbook and ran to the man who had collared my man.

"It's too late baby. Your money is no good. Even if you

had every cent, Sugar wants to make an example of him." I was livid.

"What can I do? Please don't kill him!" I was pleading with Stanford now. As much as I hated him right now the last thing I wanted was to have his blood on my hands.

The other man who had been silent walked up behind me and put his hands on my behind and rubbed real smooth then he smacked it.

"Well if you want to work off his money baby that can be arranged. It won't stop us from taking him, but it will keep us from killing him." I looked over at Stanford and saw that they had tied his hands and punched his face in so many times that his right eye had swollen shut. I felt sorry for him.

"What do you want me to do?" I'm not sure what I thought "working" for them would entail, but I was willing to help out a friend. As of that moment, he was no longer my man. I would help him get back on his feet and send him on his way. I can't lose my life trying to save his. I learned my lesson long ago when I was dealing with this crack head. He used to tell me all these lies and steal from me while I was slowly sinking to his level. I remember sitting on the side of my bed while he was free basing, and he dropped a rock. I picked it up and inspected it. I wondered what it was like. I wanted to know this mistress that had changed a healthy, vibrant, hard working man into the zombie that was leaning in front of me this instance. I rolled that demon around in my hand for a few seconds and the turned it over to its lover.

"Thank you so much baby. I know you love me." He quickly snatched it up and like our relationship it went up into smoke. After all we had been thru, he chose this as my proof of love for him. I left that night with just a bag and what clothes I had on my back. I never looked back.

"Well let me think about that sweet thang and I will get back to you. In the meantime Stan the Man has to come with us." He laughed a wicked laugh and as he snatched Stanford to his feet punched him in his stomach.

"Don't!" I yelled. I couldn't stand to see him being treated so badly. I would do anything to help him. As they walked out of my house the other gangster blew me a kiss.

I began to look around my house and saw how ram shackled it was. They had rummaged thru everything important to me. They had broken several precious crystal pieces. I thought to myself that they weren't very bright, because this place was loaded with expensive artifacts. I guess they were not here to curate the place, but to collect a debt.

Several days had passed since I heard anything about Stanford. I was feverishly watching the news in case they changed their minds about letting him live. What is it that I could possibly do to pay them back? I know I won't be getting involved with drugs. Who knows what kind of mess this man has gotten us into.

My stomach rumbles and I realize that I haven't eaten anything all day. I go into the kitchen and get some vegetables from the crisper and some sesame oil from the cupboard. I go to the freezer and look for some shrimp, when I hear the door buzzer. It was one of those gangsters. I guess he has come to tell me how I can get us out of all this mess Stanford has gotten us in. I almost didn't answer the door, but I figured I might as well face this and get it over with. Besides, they might not take the hint and just go away.

"Hey pretty lady. You ready to talk business." He didn't waste any time. I guess this was as good a time as any to make myself clear.

"Listen, I'm not getting involved in any drug deals nor am I stealing from anybody. So make you little proposition and get the hell out of my house!" I grew some balls right quick like. He grabbed me by my arm and flung me down on the sofa.

"Look bitch, you gon' do whatever the hell we tell you to." He looked me square in the eye and then gave that same wicked smile as before. "Especially if you don't want anything to happen to your little boyfriend."

"He's not my man. I don't want his ass no more. I just said I would help him out and then send him on his way." I was hoping this would seem like I was not interested in him and they would leave us alone, but I don't think he was buying it.

"Your *friend* is into us for 20 grand and we just can't let him walk away from that." He started looking around the room sizing up my possessions.

"What exactly does he owe you for?" I could have written him a check for that and gotten rid of that loser, but I needed to know what I was bailing the other loser out of.

"He likes the ponies, but they don't like him. He also has a taste for nose candy." I felt as if I could throw up. I thought I knew him. What is it about me that attracts these junkies? I went to my purse and decided against it.

"I'm sorry but he is on his own. I refuse to foot the bill for his habits. Now if you will get the hell out of here, I can finish my dinner." I was walking towards the door when this bastard grabbed me by the throat and slammed me up against the wall.

"Too late to walk away now bitch. His debt is your debt. You owe Sugar too and believe he is going to get his." I wrestled out of his grip and made a bee-line for my purse. I wrote him a check for the amount and threw it at him. He grabbed me by my hair and made me pick it up and hand it to him. I had to get this fool out of my house and out of my life as quick as possible.

"Now just for that, I'ma have to get me a little tip." He didn't waste any time pushing me over the back of the sofa and ripping off my panties. He was so rough with me all I felt was pain. He jammed himself into several times and then flipped me around and squirted his dirt on my face and hair. Bastard. I was afraid to say anything else because of what he might do to me. I just wanted him gone and the memory of Stanford erased from my life.

"Too bad you paid up. That's some prime pune. We could have worked something out." He zipped up his pants and looked at that check. He then blew me a kiss as I tried to put myself back together. He walked out the door without even closing it. I ran to shut him out and put on the dead bolts. I needed to feel secure. I'm just glad it's over.

The firm where I worked was finishing a large project and I had to stay later and finish some paperwork. When I finally had a breaking moment I went downstairs to the employee lounge to get a cup of coffee. As I was placing the caramel vanilla latte cup in the machine, I notice someone who looks exactly like Stanford talking to that blonde I saw a few weeks back. They were in the park near the fountain and he looked like he was passing her a small package. I forget all about my coffee and head back to my office to grab my purse. I locate my checkbook and place a call to my bank. As I listen to the automated voice tell me that I had a zero balance, I drop the receiver and fall back in my chair. That's why that chick was following me that day. Those cons had probably been casing me for a while. I had been had. There was no gambling or coke debt, just me being made a fool of.

I gathered my composure and called the police. I told them all that had happened and how I had come to be defrauded. They explained to me there was very little they could do for me since I willingly gave them my information and allowed him into my finances. There was not much hope for me, but I hope that in sharing my story, you will see that you can't buy love. Don't make yourself vulnerable to a man because he makes you feel good. Investigate who he says he is. If I had done that, maybe I wouldn't be starting my life over again.

The Players...

A player is one whose name suggests his role. He plays with women's feelings and wipes his feet on their heart.

A player is a man who uses the tactic of defragmentation to wrangle his harem. Although he is sweet and charming, he is totally narcissistic. He could care less about the women he abuses emotionally. He has left a trail of scars and each is a trophy on his mantle.

Defragmentation is a scattering of information, such as a childhood memory, a personal story, or a traumatic episode and then out of the blue he cuts her off. The thing about defragmentation is that most of the time he is not lying about how bad he has or will have it. This automatically wins her trust and she is blinded by his faux humility.

After he has gotten in her head and her panties, he just shuts down and leaves her without notice.

Now women cannot stand incomplete, open ended situations, so they use their imaginations and fill in the blank. Most of the time these figments of their imagination are played out with her as his heroine and it becomes her duty to save him from whatever torture he has endured up until he met her.

This strategy allows him to emotionally ravage her and take advantage of her physically. He is so slick with it that he has other women jumping thru the same hoops and telling them the same lies. This tactic is so successful because nine times out of ten, the player is a skilled lover… he could lead a woman's body to total screaming abandon.

PLAYERS

IN ORDER TO SAVE MONEY for school, I moved into a boarding house. Miss Maggie was known throughout the neighborhood for her baking skills. She made the most delicious buttermilk pound cakes you have ever tasted. Baking was a way to help her focus and stay active because she had altziemer's disease and she needed nursing care. Her son, who was an engineer, was in the process of developing a neat contraption like an auto-timing stove because it was rumored that she burned down her last home after she forgot she was making a cake. Until then they would have to settle for in house nursing.

Of all the things she accomplished, Miss Maggie had some very industrious off spring. One son was an engineer, another a doctor and she had a daughter in education. Her daughter Amy London was my high school guidance counselor and she knew that I would be a perfect match for their needs. In lieu of rent they gave me opportunity to assist Miss Maggie with her day to day needs. Like making her meals and keeping the place tidy. Some would have shied away from the idea, but that money helped me gather quite a savings my first year in college.

By year two I had a car, quite a wardrobe and was able to go on a trip to Europe with the gospel choir. I thought about getting my own apartment, but this was working so well. If it ain't broke then don't fix it.

One day as I was making breakfast, I hear the back door open and close. I call out to Miss Maggie. She didn't answer. I quickly turn off the stove and rush to the dining room. When I get in there, I see kneeling next to her the one of the most handsome men I have ever seen.

"Julie, this is my nephew Arthur. He comes and stays with me from time to time." She then gave him a peck on the cheek.

"Hi." I wipe my hands on my apron.

"Hello." He took my hand and cupped in both of his. I tried to pull away, but he held on and gave me a thirsty look while he licked his lips. This kind of made me angry. Who did he think he was? He is handsome and all, but he's not my type.

"I'm making breakfast will you join us." I asked more out of obligation than interest in his company. His arrogance was already becoming a thorn in my side and I had only known him for a few minutes. I retreat to the kitchen before he could accept or decline.

As I was getting some eggs from the refrigerator, I feel these hands slip around my waist. I quickly turn prepared to slap the piss out of this guy when he met my lips with his. He kissed me passionately as I struggled to get away. He gripped my bottom and massaged it with the same hunger I saw in his eyes in the dining room. I finally break free from this masher.

"Who the hell do you think you are?" I push him further away from me. He laughs and walks away. I hate to admit it, but he stirred something in me. He ends up back in the dining room with Ms. Maggie.

"So Aunt Maggie, you gone hook me up with one of

those cakes today?" he asked in the same arrogance as he just kissed me in the kitchen.

"Bobby where you been? You know daddy don't like it when you come in late. He gone be mad at you for sure." She was having one of her bad moments

"No Auntie it's me Arthur." He said as if she were losing her hearing. I thought to myself she's losing her memory not her hearing you idiot. He takes her hand and rubs her shoulders as she looks at him. Seeing him like this kind of takes the sting out of his molesting me in the kitchen.

"Arthur?" She was trying with all her might to remember who he was. Then she settled in her chair. He came into the kitchen and maneuvered around me as if I wasn't there. He got her a glass of juice and then began to peruse the many bottles of pills she had on the counter until he found the right one. He then rushed back into the dining room and gently attended to his aunt.

"Come on Auntie, let me feed you." I had finished making breakfast and had begun to set the table. He took her by the hand and led her to a chair. He placed a scoop of grits on a plate and took two pieces of bacon. He began to put some grape jelly on her toast just as I was bringing in the eggs.

"Bobby you know I don't like no sweet eggs." She said pushing away the plate.

"I know Auntie. I won't let the jelly touch them. You want some coffee?" He looked back at me and ordered me to bring her a cup as if he were eating in Mel's diner or something. I resisted the urge to pour it in his lap after I returned to the table. I took my time setting up the beverage tray. I hope in her stupor she remembers that she only takes cream. Just the same I put the sugar cubes on the tray to avoid making a second trip.

When I got back to the table, I saw this moment ago monster, gently spoon feeding his aunt as if she were a helpless child. My heart melted and he seemed almost human. He also seemed pretty cute. I took my place at the table and ate my food in silence. I didn't want to interrupt their moment.

After breakfast was done, I began my morning ritual of cleaning. Since Arthur was still in the dining room with his aunt, I started in the bedrooms and tried to work my way to the front of the house. I went into Miss Maggie's room to make her bed. It looked as if I hadn't cleaned in there in a month. I swear sometimes she was just like a little child. She had apparently gotten up in the middle of the night and began trying on clothes or something because clean panties bras were everywhere. Her closet was in shambles and shoes were strewn from the closet door to the bathroom floor. And here I thought this was going to be an easy day. I sucked up my aggravation and did my job. It's days like this I really think about getting my own apartment.

"She's quite a handful." I turn around and see Arthur watching me from the bedroom door.

"Yes, but I don't mind. She's a sweetheart and this helps me out." I continued to work and not even look in his direction. I was trying not to allow him into my aura. I fall so easily and it is always the same type of man. Good looking, shallow, and unstable. I flashback in my mind to him sitting at the table feeding his senile aunt and I think just maybe... nah!!! The fact that I am even considering him tells me he is no good and besides that jackal harassed me and barely even knew my name. He did have some soft lips though. I shake off these feelings as I change Miss Maggie's soiled sheets.

"You are a good woman. I wish had someone like you. I'm sorry about what happened in the kitchen. It's just in my line of work, I don't get to see beautiful women to often and I don't know how to act." I looked over to see if he was for real and found myself gazing into two of the deepest eyes I have ever seen.

"What is it that you do?" I was not going to get sucked into this game.

"I'm in the CIA." He looked over his shoulders as if someone were following him.

"Really? Is that why I have never seen you before now?' I had been living here for almost two years and this is the first I have ever heard of an Arthur much less…ooooh. It made perfect sense to me. He has to lead an undercover life and that's why no one talks about him. I wonder if he has told me too much. Only me and Miss Maggie lives here. What if someone comes after him?

"Are you on a mission now?' I asked like a little school girl. I wondered if I sounded like one of those groupies.

"No. I'm in between jobs now, so I thought I would come to town and see my favorite aunt." He answered in a relieved tone of voice. I wasn't prepared for what happened next. He came over and began to assist me in my duties. He was as attentive to the chores as he was to his Aunt Maggie.

"You thirsty?" He asked as he went to the cupboard for some glasses. We had finished all of the day's requirements and Miss Maggie was down for a nap. I was about to retreat to the basement when Arthur asked me this. Why didn't I just go on and start studying? I spent the next two hours listening to these fabulous stories that would have made James Bond seem like Urkel. Without warning he waltzed over and kissed me again. He had the softest lips and his goatee rubbed my face just right. He then retreated to the other side of the room and continued to wow me with his life experiences.

"So tell me about you." I went in on where and how I was raised. Before I could finish my history he had covered my mouth with his and began tonguing me down. I had lost this fight. He smelled so good and he felt even better than that. I loved that he wanted me. His touch was sending chills up

25

and down my spine and putting tingles in my womanhood. I don't even know this guy, but this feels so right. I thought that this kiss would end just like the others but he kept going. He gently lay me down and began to touch my body. He then looked me square in the eye and began to charm me like a snake.

I tried to refuse, but he wasn't have any of that.

"Don't stop me." He ordered. I continued on our path out of fear and obligation more so than desire. It's like I couldn't stop this. It was destined to happen.

I was a virgin. I had never known the warmth of a man and this was all new to me. I thought that you could just stop petting or kissing and the feeling would go away. That's how it worked in the past. I have had some close calls in the past and I have always been able to stop them from happening. This time was different.

By this time, my skirt was raised and so was my top and he was pawing and gnawing me as if I were a chew toy. He eased off my panties and his pants in one smoothe motion. As he lay on top of me, I could feel the bulge in his pants. It never dawned on me what was taking place until he began dry humping and tonguing me at the same time.

"Please…no…I…" He pushed my arms down by my side. I was too weak to resist him any further and before I could make another stand he eased his boxers down and slid his penis into me. I screamed in pain, hoping this would make him stop, but it only egged him on. He realized that he was breaking me in so his strokes got softer and shorter. He stopped just to ask me a question.

"Why didn't you tell me this was your first time?" Then he proceeded to grind me. "This is the only way." He slow stroked his way until all of him was inside of me. He put me in all kinds of positions; stripping away more of our clothes as we danced.

By the time he finished with me, my lady parts had been pulverized and I couldn't even stand. I was trembling with pleasure and pain. I was done for, but I wanted him to do it again.

He got up and went to the bathroom and got a warm clothe. He put it on the right spot to clean our juices and my blood off of me. It felt like acid was scalding me.

"Dang what is that sand paper?" I asked him writhing in pain.

"Naw. It's just a little rough the first time. You will get used to it." He winked at me. He then took me in his arms and held me. He was just as gentle with me as he was with his aunt. I could get used to this type of love.

"So where do we go from here lady?" He kissed me on the forehead and rubbed my shoulders. I had made plans to save that special part of myself for the man that I married. I guess he was asking me what I wanted to do.

"I was looking forward to saving my virginity for my husband, so I guess we should be getting married." Then I laughed to ease the tension I suddenly saw in his face and soften the blow of his answer.

"Baby you are right. What if I moved in here with you and Aunt Maggie? We could take care of her together and you can finish you schooling. It will be just me and you boo." I liked that idea. I was willing to go along with that.

"I'm going to call human resources department tomorrow and add you to my insurance. I want to make sure my baby is taken care of if anything happens to me." He kissed me on the lips this time.

"Can we get our own place?" I was getting used to the idea of him being around all ready.

"Yes baby, we can." He then pulled me even closer to him and began to massage my breasts. "First I'm going to finish building this bridge. Come here."

We had a repeat of our first love making session, but this time it went a little smoother than the last. I was really digging this and couldn't wait to do it again. He had me hooked on that body of his. He was an excellent lover and because he was my first, I can honestly say he was the best I had ever had.

He got up and got dressed. I lay there for a few minutes, trying to gather my strength. Eventually I nodded off. When I awoke I heard Miss Maggie calling my name. I quickly ran upstairs to check on her to see if I could be of any assistance. When I got up there she had soiled her bed and needed to be changed. I got her all cleaned up and sat her at the dining room table. It was well past her lunch time, so I began to cook dinner.

"Julie, did Arthur come over here this morning?" She was back to her normal self.

"Yes ma'am. " I smiled at the thought of him. I wanted to tell her that he was going to move in here with us and take care of us both. I was so happy.

"Be careful baby. He is my nephew and I love him, but that boy ain't no good." She leaned back in her chair. She must still be going in and out of senility. How can she say that about Arthur? From what he has told me, I couldn't have asked for a better man if I prayed for one. He was successful and good looking what more could I have asked for.

"Yes ma'am, I will." I just let it go. She will see when he moves in and takes charge.

"I know he is a nice looking young man, but he got too many chil'ren for a respectable young lady like yourself to be messing with." What was she talking about he didn't mention any children. It must be time for her medicine.

"Miss Maggie have you taken your pills yet?" I needed to change this subject quickly. There is no way I gave my most precious possession to a dead beat. What about all that sweet talk and future planning we just did? I couldn't be another notch on his belt.

"That's why his last wife left him. He had too much baby mama drama going on. He got almost 10 children by six different women and he ain't taking care of none of them. The only reason he comes around here is to get some money or to hide out from that woman he's living with. I gave him 50 bucks and sent him on his way. Did he hit on you for any money?" She asked looking me in the eye.

"No ma'am." I wanted to tell her he took something more precious from me than gold. Something I will never be able to get back. After I made her dinner and got her situated, I went down in the basement and lay down across that crime scene I called a bed. I looked across the room at my purse. Dare I go and see what I already knew? Naw; I will just lay here and pray for a negative HIV and pregnancy test.

...and the
Virtue Slayers

A virtue slayer is a horse of a different color. This creature has every intention of fulfilling his vows and making good on his promises, but there is just one thing standing in his way: his nature.

This man has issues that keep him on the lamb. He is usually addicted to drugs, has perverse sexual proclivities, or he is morally depraved. He is like a spiritual vampire that drains all of the life from an unsuspecting, almost always virtuous woman.

Whoa be tide the creature that crosses his path and falls into his net. He is the hardest of the three to leave and the easiest to fall in love with. I have seen the best of women fall under his spell.

THE VIRTUE SLAYERS

"THAT IS A BEAUTIFUL SUIT!" exclaimed Mother Ledbetter. She and I had similar tastes in clothes. After all, there are only so many styles a woman of sanctification can sport. That is why so many women in the church try to out dress each other on Sundays.

"Thank you. Yours isn't too bad either." We have often come to services wearing the same styles just different colors. There is this one suit that we both possess with diamond covered buttons and a flare tail skirt. Her's is platinum and mine is a soft lilac. I am not one for bright colors, but every now and again. I go all out. I am a dead ringer for Tamela Mann, but I have long blonde hair. This makes me a target not only for single men, but a few married ones have made advances on me. Single men are only interested until they find out that I am celibate and married men get the hint after I tell them that I am going to make sure their wives find out what a letch they married.

I will admit that it is hard holding on to my vow, but I want to make sure I give my husband something very few have had access to. No, I am not a virgin, but I am putting some distance between me and the last physical relationship. He was our youth minister. He had testified many times that he wanted a wife and that the Lord had promised him that he would marry me. Things were going well until he was caught in the bed with another man. I got tested for months after things fell thru with him. I went ahead and allowed him into my body because I believed that he was mine.

Another time, I was corresponding with this brother I thought was righteous and had integrity, but he was just like all the others. I can't remember how he got to be a part of my circle, and truth be told he was not my type. He was intelligent and very talented, but he was old; not just in age, but in his demeanor. When I saw him I perceived that he had good intentions, but that soon shorted out. He would send me tidbits of songs he had created in the past and all of these facts that really were of no interest to me. Out of respect I would say something like "Wow!" or "That's great!" When I should have been saying "Buzz off!" or "Don't you have something better to do with your time?"

Well after about seven months of interaction he finally breaks down and sends me this email stating how sweet he thought I was and how he respected me too much to say anything remotely flirtatious to me. He called me a WOG or woman of God and ended it with these wonderful blessings. It took me a while to respond because my internet connection stinks. Sometimes I can't logon for hours. This time it was in my best interest. I simply said I was flattered, called him a gentleman for his respect, and returned those same blessings. Two days later he sent me another one of those corny information bytes under some woman named Dotsy. Then he attempts to start a conversation with me and her at the same time. I just logged off. He was so obvious. He was hoping I was one of those church ladies who was so desperate for attention that they would succumb to premarital relations and sacrifice their virtue. Ehhhh!....Wrong answer! So now he has to retract his interest by flaunting his relationship with this other woman in my face. He should've just asked me. I would have told her you just did me a favor. Now I don't have to settle for a Bill Cosby look-alike with no money.

Another joker that came to me was a whole lot smoother. We corresponded for few weeks and then he said that he couldn't live without me. His heart was in pure anguish because he had never met such a beautiful and gracious creature as me. He told me that he was an engineer who worked off the coast of Scotland on an oil rig and he was thinking about moving back to the states to settle down. He sent these beautiful poems and love sonnets to me daily. I was beginning to fall for his bullshits until he asked me to book his trip to my town. The love filled scales fell off my eyes. He disappeared offline for a few days and then comes back online claiming that he had been waiting for me to log in so he contacted one of my class mates. Mind you it was one of the least attractive of them all. She was obnoxious and a bit of a bully. Perfect for what he was trying to achieve. He was probably an inmate looking for a place to lay his head when he got out of jail. All I know is I was not going out like that.

Now the one who finally landed me was different from them all. He appeared to be respectable and he totally ignored me. I caught him checking me out a few times and I tried to use it to my advantage. I began to dress like a first lady, because that was my aim. I wanted to be his wife. He was a minister in training and I knew he would make a great pastor.

At first he called me incessantly. Every day for a month, he called me two or three times. When he wasn't calling he was texting. I got kind of lazy and stopped auditioning for the roll when he didn't move in my time. I finally got tired of waiting and asked him out. A shocking turn of events made this an impossible situation to leave.

He came right and said "Look sis, I am not interested in you that way." BINGO! I was hooked completely. It was my mission to make this man fall helplessly in love with me. It worked. He did and now I am getting ready to say 'I do'.

OUR WEDDING DAY

"Baby I like this color." He had taken an interest in everything from my hair color to my manicure/pedicure. I slimmed down 20lbs because he wanted to take me to Barbados for our honeymoon and he felt I would look cuter in my bathing suit. He was the perfect gentleman. I never had to worry about what we were going to do for the weekends. He was so thoughtful and attentive that I could count on his plans like clockwork.

It was an autumn red hair color. It was a little bright for my taste but, he had to look at me so I figured if he approved then I better go ahead and get it done. Besides, I was raised old school. You did things that pleased your husband. If it would make him happy, it was your job as his woman to make it so. I was happy to be his lady. All of the other women in the church would have given their right arm to be in my shoes. I must admit I enjoyed being the object of their envy. Especially after he got down on one knee in the midst of the congregation and proposed to me. I was shocked and elated that my dream of being a wife had finally come true.

"All done ma'am." The shampoo tech was very gentle when she wiped the water from my forehead. I slowly adjusted my eyes and turned my head towards the light to get a better glimpse of my new hue. With my color and hazel eyes, this just might work. The longer I stared at it the more I liked it. He was right. I couldn't wait until he saw me.

"Wow!" I was impressed with the job well done. She took her time rolling and sitting me under the dryer. I checked my text messages and he had sent me an 'I love you message'. I got those 3 or 4 times a day. He was my dark gable. He was always talking about our future.

Our big day was at hand and the makeover he so carefully planned went over without a hitch. I was looking better than

I had in years and I felt like I was walking on clouds. I had a fine man who thought I was the center of the universe and we had a wonderful future together. To top off all of my new digs, his father purchased a new car for us as a wedding present. He already owned his house and he was going to start his own business once we got situated in our marriage. We had it made. Things couldn't have been any better if I had planned them.

On the day of our wedding, I had the jitters. Not the normal 'I can't believe I'm finally getting married' jitters, but the 'I think something is wrong' jitters. I walk back to the Sunday school rooms where the ladies were dressing to escort me down the aisle. I think they were more excited than me. I picked a small corner of the room and began to pray. I wasn't sure what to say, but I needed to make contact with God. No words came to mind so I just sat there and meditated on His love for me until I felt better.

"We have got to get you in this gown girl!" That was the wedding planner. She did an awesome job at making this event what it was. Most of the ideas were Major's though. That's my fiancé. He put just as much effort into this wedding as she did. Maybe that's what my problem is. I'm not sure what to expect when I go down that aisle. From looking at this beautiful gown, I'm definitely going to be queen for a day.

"Take your places ladies! Remember when you reach the 3rd row wait for your escort to take you the rest of the way to the altar." I can hardly wait to see how this is all going to go down. My prince charming has gone all out to make this my special day and I can't wait until we can celebrate together.

As the music begins to play, the butterflies return to my stomach. I want to stop this wedding because I just now realized that it is not what I want, but what someone else wants for me. I'm not sure I even love Major. Come to think of it; it wasn't my idea to even start dating him. It was just offered to me and I was too weak to say no.

"It's time Yolanda." She may as well have been leading me to the electric chair. I felt lightheaded. It was as if someone had sucked all the air out of the room. I made it to the foyer and once the doors of the sanctuary opened, I saw the flowers and all the lace that made this fairy tale complete. In my eyes, the only thing that was missing from this scene was the casket.

THE HONEYMOON IS OVER...

"Where do you think you are going?" He won't let me go anywhere without giving me a hard time. It's always an argument or some kind of conflict when I want to do something. He's no longer the sweet man who I met a year ago. He is now the warden who is long from pardoning me from being his wife.

After the wedding, we were so in love it was almost painful to be apart from him. Now I can hardly wait until he goes to work just to get some time to myself. He has become so obsessive until I feel stifled. I have to ask him for money, because he didn't want his wife to work. I have to ask his permission to go or do anything that doesn't involve him. Even if he let's me go, when I return he makes me take off my panties to smell them to see if I have done anything with anyone else. Once during the Super bowl I went to get the refreshments for him and his friends, when I returned he had kicked them all out.

"What happened to the party?" He looked at me like it was my fault.

"Why you have to walk around here in those tight clothes? You act like a ho' sometimes." This man was going to be the death of me. I had long since stopped paying attention when he went on these insecure rants of his. He scares me sometimes with his innuendo. I know what a jealous mate can be capable of. If only I had followed my first mind and left him at the altar.

I remember that day I signed up for this abuse like it was yesterday. After I made it to the altar, the preacher look at us both and asked the congregation if there was any just cause that anyone could see why we shouldn't be joined as man and wife. I wanted to yell with all my might, "ME!"

I didn't love him then and I have only come to tolerate him now. The only reason we are still together is because he is finally the head minister of a local church. I am finally living out my dream of being a first lady. I have to represent what is holy. Even though I am dying inside, I still have to let my light shine.

To ease the guilt of living this lie, I drink. It's not a problem or anything and I can stop anytime I want to, but I need it to get through those endless services where I look at the bane of my existence and see what my life could have been if I had not married this man. I should have waited on the Lord to send me my "him" instead of going out there and getting him myself. This may be my punishment for getting ahead of God's will. Who knows maybe one day we will be able to get past my initial disgust of him and become the man and woman of God we should be, but until then I will just have to suffer.